Reflective Rising

Poetry & Prose

Written By: Taylor Jean

Reflective Rising by Taylor Jean

Through reflection, I rise.

Reflective Rising by Taylor Jean

It's messy in here; my mind.
It's dark in here, but I cry out light.
I try to free myself with a rhyme.
The clock echoes in my thoughts;
I am nothing but a product of Time.
Words tend to find me most at midnight.
I am a shadow of haunted chaos in flight.
Welcome, to this mess of my mind;
Where ghostly lovers dance in the twilight.
Where I seek to make everything right.
Where I long to return to a fleeting moment.
Where I bleed out my secrets and hold it;
Hold it all in...
Until my fingertips reach the pen.

Reflective Rising by Taylor Jean

I feel weak from time to time.
Like breathing is just too much.
When this happens, I like to rhyme.
It is with words that my Soul is touched.
Talking about it was never for me.
So, I write it down on paper.
This way, pain and love
Emanate freely through me.
These words carry parts of my Soul;
A sacred, dissipating vapor.

Reflective Rising by Taylor Jean

I may not be able to flick my truth
off of the tip of my tongue, but I can
bleed it out in ink through the tip of my pen.

Reflective Rising by Taylor Jean

Love is how we forget time;
poetry is how we eternalize it.

Reflective Rising by Taylor Jean

Lunacy finds me,
Only when Time cannot;
To write.

Reflective Rising by Taylor Jean

This is maddening.
I cannot stop writing.
Thoughts are spinning.
No choice, but to alchemize
all that got caught
within my eyes.
It's how I start
my new beginning.
It's how I, persistently,
keep on winning.
The veil never stops thinning.
Words tremble so hard
within these bones
that I must externalize
all of my sinning.
Maddening, it is;
these thoughts
shake my rib cage
for freedom.

Reflective Rising by Taylor Jean

There is such a fine, florescent line drawn between utter madness and free creativity.

Reflective Rising by Taylor Jean

I'll
　drip...
　　drop...
　a little bit of
　　　melancholia,
　　so that you
　can see what
　　it's like inside
　　　these veins.

Reflective Rising by Taylor Jean

Gotta worry about
What's to come,
Or even what never will.

Gotta form all of these ideas;
Let all that I should have said,
Runneth over and spill.

Gotta let all the "would'ves,"
"Could'ves," and "should'ves"
Crawl into this heart; make it beat faster.

Gotta bow down to my knees,
Beg for mercy from this anxiety;
Treat it as my everlasting Master.

Reflective Rising by Taylor Jean

Every yesterday, I think of tomorrow.
Presence has fled this flesh.

Reflective Rising by Taylor Jean

Lately, my ambition gets ahead of me.
My heart beats faster, in effort to
Keep up with the pace of my goals.
There is this constant need for achievement.
Meanwhile, I've said my goodbyes to an old self
And I could just use some time for bereavement.

Reflective Rising by Taylor Jean

I can't help but wonder what
it would be like, living in a body
with no anxiety who's made
a home inside of its bones.

Reflective Rising by Taylor Jean

Five steps forward,
And ten steps back.
Wish the stars above
Would just cut me some slack.

I've been trying to rise above it;
The defiant aches of anguish.
Been bruising all of this skin,
Trying to find a way to vanquish.

My bones are cracking,
Heart is shattering.
Mind is splitting.
Soul is lacking.

I just keep reaching…
For something intangible,
But the intangibility only
Brings me a depriving inevitability.

Reflective Rising by Taylor Jean

I sit here and talk to
Someone I cannot see.
I plead for redemption;
Adjust my blood to
Flow at their speed.

Somehow I am always
Brought back to this room,
Talking to Someone that
The stars have consumed.

I ask for different, while knowing
My worth and the pain that
Brought me to this space.
Yet, my desires always end up
Gone without a trace.

So, I walk with grace;
In hopes of encouragement
From the essence of inevitability.
But even that brings me right back here,
Talking to a Someone I cannot see.

Reflective Rising by Taylor Jean

I'm so caught up in the
Strings of what could be.
I'm tangled with intangibility.
My dreams might be the death of me.
If only all of the others could see,
Even if just for a moment.

Reflective Rising by Taylor Jean

Falling apart is an art of mine;
Exceedingly wonderful with a
Convincing, "Oh, yeah, I'm fine."

Reflective Rising by Taylor Jean

I feel lost these days;
As if I'm doing something wrong.
Like I keep pulling away from myself,
While having no idea when I'm doing so.
Until it's too late...
Until I've changed something
That never should have changed.
I know, it sounds pitiful.
I understand change is the
Only constant in life, but regardless
I feel like I messed something up.
Like I'm on the wrong path, suddenly.
Like I altered the winding roads of my Soul.
The truth, the answers;
They're tickling my insides.
It's this tingling of intangible knowing.
All I want is for it to find my heart,
And to begin glowing; illuminating
Where it is, I must go.
What it is, I must do.
But here I am, and I have no fricken clue.

Reflective Rising by Taylor Jean

Stress up to the skies,
Glossing over my eyes.
Silent, trembling cries
That keep me awake.

Regrets down to my toes.
Grief, with the wind, it blows
Into my dying lungs.
All of my air, it takes.

Loneliness deep in my veins,
Creating immortal pains;
A collision of trains
Crashing into my Soul.

The darkness has come.
I hear its forceful drum;
To it, I must succumb.
Wherever will I be forged to go?

Reflective Rising by Taylor Jean

The skies broke apart
Along with my heart.
The clouds rained
Down with my tears.
The world set ablaze,
In the wickedest of ways;
An earth destroyed
By all of my fears.

Reflective Rising by Taylor Jean

My head is rushed.
My breath is breathless.
I'm running.
I'm hiding.
My worry is endless.
Emotions in a bottle,
Leaving me changeless.
Afraid of my own potential.
Even more so of it going wasted.
I tasted— the honey of hope.
I swallowed it, but
Never learned to cope.
I'm hanging by an old
And tattered rope.
All I want to know;
Will they'll be telling
The tale of how I had
Fallen?

Reflective Rising by Taylor Jean

I always try to build a less
chaotic version of myself,
but it all just crumbles
down every time.

Reflective Rising by Taylor Jean

I've outgrown this,
Where is my new pot?
I've worked hard for this,
I can no longer rot.

What more can I do?
I have run out of room.
This is, surely, a sign that
This soil's gone gloom.

Am I fated for doom?
I can no longer consume
All of the stagnant and rancid
Dressed up in costume.

I need oxygen, and Sun.
I don't deserve this ache to run.
My stem can't hold me up;
I'm bearing the weight of what's to come.

I've grown weak from
All of this pleading.
My leaves will, soon,
Start bleeding.

My time for flourish is fleeting.
My petals have begun depleting.
Just a little more room is all
This Soul is needing.

Just have a little mercy,
Is that really such a cheating?
My roots have grown numb
From this goddamned repeating.

Reflective Rising by Taylor Jean

I don't know what it is with me.
These moods, this heart;
They ache inside of me.
I'm tired of making my way out of it,
Just to fall right back in again.
I yearn for a day that I am steady.

Reflective Rising by Taylor Jean

It's just been a lot; living.
I don't know much longer
I can go on breathing.
It's like everything that
Has ever given me hope,
Just keeps on leaving.
I'm bleeding...
Dripping out of me, is
Everything that would
Keep me going.
My bones have
Become so fragile.
My heart tries to escape,
Pounding so obtrusively.
My brain has covered
Reality with a gray haze.
Is there a way...
Out of here?
My Soul is, surely,
Searching for it.
I hear the cries of dusk
And the heartbeat of mourn
In my plangent dreams.
When will these vile veins
Have seethed the way
Toward the end of my means?

Reflective Rising by Taylor Jean

Passion is merging with monotony.
I'm beginning to lose grip on my integrity.
How could purpose feel redundant?
Is it my own fear of becoming abundant?

Doing things as I'm told
Is beginning to feel so old.
My enthusiasm is growing mold.
My reasons are turning cold.

It feels as if I've fogged the vision of my Soul.
My mind and heart are split, not whole.
What exactly is my ultimate goal?
How could I feel empty doing things
That once made me feel full?

I'm bored with all that once would excite me.
Zestfulness has grown a dull reality.
Who is it that I truly want to be?
I thought I had it figured out, but I guess
No one can know of their own destiny.

Reflective Rising by Taylor Jean

Grumpiness, it's like a hunger pain.
Need to feed it, will it go away?
The darkness within is stirring.
I'm a boiling pot. I'm a lion purring.
No light makes it inside of this den.
So, with the heart of a lion, I write with this pen.
Fight or flee, it's all that's on my mind.
It's contentment I seek,
But may never find.

Reflective Rising by Taylor Jean

I'm just another nothing
who feels everything.

Reflective Rising by Taylor Jean

My Soul swallows the depths of everything, while everyone else just seems to float upon the surface with all of their senses drowning below.

Reflective Rising by Taylor Jean

My heart grew, thicker
As the space got, bigger.
I don't know which way, is up.
Maybe,
    I'll
        Just
            Fall...
                Deeper.

Reflective Rising by Taylor Jean

I'm sinking deeper into
All that I wish I was not.
I've never felt like the
right amount of human.
I've always felt like a lot.
Something about the way I am,
Seems to scare people away.
There is a darkness in my heart
That never wants to see the light of day.
I cannot help it, but that's not what
all of the shallow people say.
If living like this was my choice,
well I chose my fate and we're
all just born to die again anyway.

Reflective Rising by Taylor Jean

I only have my own arms to fall into,
and they're hollow,
so I fall right through myself
each time that I seek consolation.

Reflective Rising by Taylor Jean

Am I here?
Can you hear me?
Can anyone see me?
I'm a forsaken echo;
Designed to be let go.
This youngster in me, is hurting.
They've been ignored so much
That they feel disturbing.
So many years I have spent, worrying.
What should I say?
What's worth their time?
Will I finally be seen one day?
Wil I ever find someone who cares
About all of these feelings that are mine?

Reflective Rising by Taylor Jean

A tender ache lives
Inside of my esophagus.
It will remain with me until
I lay in my sarcophagus.

The truths that I never spoke,
Will haunt beside the undead.
They'll cradle me to the Moon,
Echoing all that I had never said.

I'll be stuck there, lonely;
Left to hear those echoes
Bleed within the stars.
All these unsaid words
Will live on, as eternal scars.

They'll befriend hope,
Tricking me to go on;
A ghost abandoned inside
Of the untouchable sky,
Beyond the break of dawn.

No one will ever know
That I am up there.
All these unsaid truths
Will rebirth me, forgotten
In the space between
Everywhere and nowhere.

Reflective Rising by Taylor Jean

I'm feeling a bit displaced;
In the wrong space.
I can't find the one in my heart.
My mind is shrouded in fog.
My bones just want to shrivel up.
I'm not sure how to get by anymore.

Reflective Rising by Taylor Jean

There used to be a party in my head.
Now it's just dead; less vibrant.
I'm a corpse dragging its
Feet around this earth.
My flesh is a toxic confinement.

Life took all of the life out of me.
Now I just float around, aimlessly.
My brain no longer holds the capacity
To analyze and interpret anything, wisely.

I've been chewed up and spit out.
Loved, while I've bled out.
Manipulated into an eternal doubt
That I'm anything more than a little
Monster with a heart of joy that can be
Stolen whenever another Soul might need it.

Reflective Rising by Taylor Jean

I drift inward,
Seemingly gaining
But truthfully losing control.
It appears as such a natural flow,
But I fight to look this graceful;
No one knows.
In my Soul, it shows.
But no one can see this light.
No one can feel my fright.
No one is with me in the dead of night.
No one knows how hard it is; surrendering.
I feel guilty, as if I'm pretending.
Though, I am not at fault for
What others cannot see or feel.
They'll perceive me in endless ways,
As I devote my movement
To the stars and heal.
I'll let it go, and be on my way.
I'll welcome a brand new me,
Confusing the minds of others,
As I hug the Sun with my breath each day.
I don't think I'd want it any other way.
As long as I've got the voice of my heart,
I can live on; free from the worry of
What they might believe or say.

Reflective Rising by Taylor Jean

Inside-out.
Turning, twisting.
Getting the truth.
Clarity of my worth.
Secrets inside of my tongue.

Reflective Rising by Taylor Jean

I think I know who I am now.
I think I'm ready to put it in front of the world.
I think I can speak up now.
I think I'm ready to bleed out every word.

Reflective Rising by Taylor Jean

Into myself, I wander.
And oh, how I do ponder;
Why am I here?
Do I carry meaning
Inside of these bones?
I look into the mirror,
And it's like someone else
Is here...
With me;
Am I ever alone?

This heavy, weightless
Feeling wraps around my
Chest as I regret all of the
Bridges I've burned.
I have no clue where
They will leave me
To join those who rest.
My world has done so
Much more than flipped,
It has turned...

Opposite;
I'm spinning backwards,
Against the time that
Has chained me to
The center of my Earth.
From birth, I have had
This incorporeal light
Illuminating the truth
Of where I receive my worth.

And it is now,
That I stand in it.
My direction,
Subject to change.
I've done more than
Write a new chapter.
I have torn out and
Burned every single page.

I'll let the ghost in my heart
Speak for the silence it's suffered.
They'll transform every word that
Lost Souls, unconsciously, uttered.
The beat of my muscle has begun
Ripping my flesh and
Developing a stutter.
Oh, but regardless, I will echo
The voices of every woman
Who had been wronged
For believing in anything other
Than what is accepted
By authorities.

Reflective Rising by Taylor Jean

My life is not peaceful right now.
There are parasites who wander.
I pray for better days.
I hope that they suffocate and die
from the pain of my need for justice;
my worthiness of a life better than this.

Reflective Rising by Taylor Jean

I don't need to get
Caught up in the idea
Of them accepting me.
They can do so, that's cool.
But if they don't,
They won't be seeing
The end of me.

I've learned all of
What I deserve.
And while they may
Have the opportunity to
Float around my life,
It will be around their
Perceptions that I swerve.

They'll ricochet back into
Their own selves, off of
My mirror-like essence.
Their assumptions and
Equations will deflect them
Right back into their very
Own aching presence.

Reflective Rising by Taylor Jean

Maybe today, I can finally
Begin to feel like I'm not just
Some character in a movie.

Maybe today, I can truly be with
What is in my life rather than
Feel like it all has no room for me.

Maybe today, is the day
That my world won't feel
So planned out and irrevocable.

Maybe today, I'll finally feel
Like I've got all of this chaos
Within and around me under control.

Reflective Rising by Taylor Jean

I have been changing.
Fluctuating.
Embracing.
Creating.
Crying.
Waiting.
Hoping.
Praying.
Elevating.
All of the things you've been saying...
Are they promises, broken?
I have been holdin' on.
What went wrong?
Can't find the Sun;
The light.
But I'll be alright.
Just know I'll always wish that
You had stayed by my side.

Reflective Rising by Taylor Jean

I guess you were just another temporary person bringing me a permanent lesson.

Reflective Rising by Taylor Jean

Some only stick around me
to become a story in ink.
But they never end up where they think.
They're in the oceans of my Soul.
Like an anchor, they sink.
And my belly grows full with all
the poison they made me drink.
Turning them into words never
rids me of their lost pieces.
Poetic creations hold permanence,
but they never result in justice.

Reflective Rising by Taylor Jean

I miss the calm; the quiet.
I long for the nights that were silent.
My heart was open; didn't have to pry it.
Now I have this ache to change what I did.

Reflective Rising by Taylor Jean

I, so badly, need some distance.
I need privacy; solitude.
I say this with conviction.
I need it in an instance.

I feel everything around me
Seeping into my skin that glistens.
I need to be separate from it, but
I seem to be the only one who listens.

It's all closing in around me;
A silent and indescribable
Claustrophobia of melancholy.
I beg for space, so solemnly.

This Soul is too big for this world.
It's become free; unfurled.
This light has swirled, and swirled.
But everything is so heavy.

It all, so viscously, squeezes me
Until every single bit of me
Has been swallowed up
And curled.

Reflective Rising by Taylor Jean

I've become one of the
quietest people I know,
and I'm not sure if it's from
all of the pain or just
a part of who I am.
Maybe I was always this way,
but life doesn't reflect so.
The silence grew into me;
veins of mute vinery.

Reflective Rising by Taylor Jean

I want to curl up
Inside of nothingness
And let everyone forget me,
So they can no longer hold
Anymore unhealthy expectancy.

Not quite sure what more
They could have from me.
I'm tired and I just want to spread
Some of this love into my arteries.

Is that too much to ask for?
I, surely, feel it's not.
Just let me be;
I'll come back, bloomed
After these bones can rot.

Reflective Rising by Taylor Jean

I want to curl up
Inside of myself,
Like I did in the
Caterpillar stage,
But I guess these
Wings are different;
They fly away all the rage.

Reflective Rising by Taylor Jean

I've been given a second chance
By the heart of fate, and I must
Make the very most out of it.
It's time to believe in myself
Like I never have before this.

It's time to trust the flutters of
The butterflies in my gut;
Follow the Sun in my heart,
As I climb my way out of this
Soul-aching, self-created rut.

Each night, I'll sit with the Moon;
Talk of how I had created such little room.
Admit to all of the things I have avoided;
A perpetual state of ignorance that
Had kept all of my peace devoided.

I'll let the stars swallow me into their light;
Allow them to cleanse me, as my
Shadow puts up a good fight.
I'll become a better me, each and every night.
I'll harness this second chance and make it right.

Reflective Rising by Taylor Jean

Within the light of day
I'll find a way to say
All of the things that keep
Bursting my neurons into
Shards of light rays.
I'll transcend all of my
Mournful days; my Soul
Dancing until the end of all days.
I'll spend all of my eternity
Creating restorative pathways.

Reflective Rising by Taylor Jean

I'm so unsure,
Making reckless decisions.
I've been cut; so sore.
Gotta sew up these incisions.

Been looking for healing
Inside of all the wrong places.
Been searching for a new me
Within all of my old faces.

I'm afraid to move
Forward alone.
I blind myself of all the truth;
How much I have, gracefully, grown.

Gotta bring my attention
Toward this breaking heart.
Gotta start fresh, with no other,
And create art out of every part.

Where will I find the courage
That all of this, so deeply, requires?
Maybe I'll try to ignite this Soul,
And find a kind of peace within the fire?

I'll bask within my flame,
Holding onto no amount of shame.
I'll reclaim my misunderstood name.
I'll come out stronger than the way I came.

Reflective Rising by Taylor Jean

Ready for new.
Ready for different.
Ready for change.
Need a break.
Need some space.
Need to rearrange.
Heart grown wild.
Soul set ablaze.
Clearing the path
Toward better days.

Reflective Rising by Taylor Jean

You can find me beyond the Sun;
I've always flown too far,
Toward the fire, to burn
Into the dancing ether.

Reflective Rising by Taylor Jean

There is a fire in my heart,
Telling me to prepare for
A brand new start.
My dreams are ready
To burst apart, and
Form miracles before me.
My imaginings have never been
What they may appear to be.
Regeneration is happening;
My bones turning to soil,
And blooming sacred peonies.
It's raining epiphanies;
My thirst quenched with
An unrecognizable power.
I'm turning light into food;
A photosynthesizing flower.
These veins, this blood, my cells…
It's all just energy.
I am reborn, transformed;
The Universe and I, a
Dancing destiny of synergy.

Reflective Rising by Taylor Jean

Within solemn ashes, I lay.
A new me, but in pain.
Remorse and grief in my veins.
Growing is beautiful, but comes with rain.

Reflective Rising by Taylor Jean

Within rose petals, I lay strewn;
A million little pieces of me,
Tucked away inside of fragile armor.

Reflective Rising by Taylor Jean

Be soft with me, please.
I am so fragile.
I am a crumbling Soul,
Trapped inside of porcelain bones.

Reflective Rising by Taylor Jean

In love and armor, I hold this
fragile heart away from any other.

Reflective Rising by Taylor Jean

I am the fog that rests upon the tree top, swiftly, swirling the essence of emotion and Soul into the air that we breathe.

Reflective Rising by Taylor Jean

Leaves fall with the grip
That I once had on myself.
Losing sanity in the winds of
Grace, I became one with
Darkness once more.
Blowing gently through
The heart of grief, I had
Solemnly sworn to leave
The door of my Soul ajar;
To look beyond the stars
That I, so dearly, adore.

Reflective Rising by Taylor Jean

I dare to wear
My imperfections as
A, weightless, sleeve.

No longer will I be
Held down by my
Heart, who grieves.

Past reflections of
Who they saw me as
Within their mirrors, shatter.

The reasonings of my Soul
Will go on, free; living as
All that truly matters.

Reflective Rising by Taylor Jean

I'm changing.
It's a bit frightening.
Also, exciting.
It's quite enticing.
I'm fascinated with something I cannot see,
But only feel.
Is any of this real?
I feel everything, although I'm numb.
What a contradiction it is; my existence.
Regardless, I'm ready to go the distance.

Reflective Rising by Taylor Jean

I am not designed for
The ways of this world.
The sounds consume me
And shatter me to pieces of
Stardust that beg for freedom.

The people confuse me and
I can't imagine a version of me
That could ever be close
To anything like them.

I came from the stars and
Everything about this land
Reminds me of how far
From home I really am.

The joy in one's heart only
Brings me back to the time
When I could actually hold that feeling
From the swirling of the galaxies;

A Soul-wrenching regret and mourn
For choosing temporary experience
Over the bliss that rests just outside
The temptation of lustful realities.

The cosmic, sacred design of me
Has no place on the grounds of mankind.
No matter how hard these flesh-driven
Vehicles may try, it will only be a
Soul of the sky that they will find.

Reflective Rising by Taylor Jean

So often, I am led back into myself.
Truth is, I am the only one who
can give myself what I need.
And I have come to learn that
I have never been selfish for falling
back into my own heart; it appears
to be the way toward a kind of gnostic liberation.
It's always watered my ever-growing Soul.
How could one not be called to such bliss?

Reflective Rising by Taylor Jean

I hold a healthy attitude
Toward the precious
Times of solitude.
They awaken me to a
Profound magnitude.
They bring to me, an
extraordinary sanctitude.

Reflective Rising by Taylor Jean

I am but a fallen leaf, floating
upon the flow of a stream;
its depths holding mirrors.

Reflective Rising by Taylor Jean

Life struck me with an event
That sent me into oblivion.
Smacked into a brick wall,
And melted into obsidian.

Can't see anything,
Don't know where to go.
Time can't even tell.
Only Death will know.

The decision wasn't mine.
I don't bear the hands of fate.
Maybe one day I'll be fine?
The breath of Unknown, sets the date.

I'll suffer in the arms of grace;
Let faith wade in these waters.
I'll allow it to take me home.
Toward relief, it sacredly charters.

Reflective Rising by Taylor Jean

There is a clamor of Souls
Inside of my heart that
Converse of fantasies;
Dancing to the beat of
This muscle and driving
These bones toward a
Blissful daydream.

Reflective Rising by Taylor Jean

Sometimes, you have to risk it all
for a dream that others would only
wake up and forget.

Reflective Rising by Taylor Jean

I finally see myself for who I am,
And not all that others are afraid to be.
I thought it was purely impossible for me
To achieve the things that filled me with
So-called, "unfathomable dreamery."
I've buried their mockery.
I've set ablaze their worry.
If this is unbelievable, then call me
The fool who knew I was worthy.

Reflective Rising by Taylor Jean

I'll remain strong.
I'll lift up high, the belief
That what I feel is not wrong.
I'll validate my emotions.
I'll whip up sadness and grief
Into invigorating potions.
I don't need to give in to
The cracks they leave on my heart.
I can seal them with gold and
Turn them into works of captivating art.
I can paint these scars with glitter;
Reflect all that they truly are within.
I can move forward in love and honor
For the space where it is that we all begin.

Reflective Rising by Taylor Jean

Made in United States
North Haven, CT
23 August 2024